796 DEV ED

GN00789401

COMMITTED
TO JUDAISM

A JEWISH COMMUNITY

CANCELLED
REMOVED FROM STOCK

SYLVIA AND BARRY
SUTCLIFFE

Development
Cooperation
Ireland
DCI Resource
Centre
1 2 JUL 2004
Bishop's Square, Redmond's Hill, Dublin 2.
Tel: 353 1 478 9400 Fax: 353 1 475 1006
Web: www.dci.gov.ie

5271

RMEP

RELIGIOUS AND MORAL EDUCATION PRESS

Religious and Moral Education Press
An imprint of Chansitor Publications Ltd,
a wholly owned subsidiary of Hymns Ancient & Modern Ltd
St Mary's Works, St Mary's Plain
Norwich, Norfolk NR3 3BH

Copyright © 1994 Sylvia and Barry Sutcliffe

Sylvia and Barry Sutcliffe have asserted their right under the
Copyright, Designs and Patents Act, 1988, to be identified as
Authors of this Work.

All rights reserved. No part of this publication may be
reproduced, stored in a retrieval system, or transmitted, in any form
or by any means, electronic, electrostatic, magnetic tape, mechanical,
photocopying, recording or otherwise, without
permission in writing from the publishers.

First published 1994

ISBN 1-85175-024-X

Acknowledgements
The Authors and Publisher would like to thank the
Management Committee and members of the United Synagogue,
Hendon, particularly those whose interviews appear in this book,
for their generous help. We are especially indebted to Nicky
Goldman, Community Director of the United Synagogue,
Hendon, for her time and care as our principal contact during
all stages of work.

We are also grateful to Frank Gent for setting up the photograph
of the Torah scroll on pages 20–21.

Designed and typeset by Topics Visual Information, Exeter

Photography by Michael Burton-Pye

Printed in Singapore by Tien Wah Press for
Chansitor Publications Ltd, Norwich

CONTENTS

INTRODUCTION

The books in this **Faith and Commitment** series give you the chance to look at religions and religious denominations (groups within religions) through the personal reflections of people with a religious commitment.

To create these books, we visited local religious communities in different parts of Britain. We talked to people across the range of ages and roles you'd expect to find in a community – parent, child, grandparent, priest, community worker. That is, we interviewed people like you and your family, your friends, the people where you live. We asked them all the same questions and we've used the themes of those questions as chapter headings in the books.

Each chapter contains extracts from those interviews. People interpret our questions as they want to. They talk freely in their own words about religious ideas and personal experiences, putting emphasis where they think it belongs for them. The result is a set of very individual insights into what religion means to some of the people who practise it. A lot of the insights are spiritual ones, so you may have had similar thoughts and experiences yourself, whether or not you consider yourself a 'religious' person.

You will see that some pages include FACT-FINDER boxes. These are linked to what people say in the interview extracts on these pages. They give you bits of back-up information, such as a definition or where to look up a reference to a prayer or a piece of scripture. Remember that these books are not textbooks. We expect you to do some research of your own when you need to. There are plenty of sources to go to and your teacher will be able to help.

There are also photographs all through the books. Some of the items you can see belong to the people whose interview extracts appear on those pages. Most of these items have personal significance. Some have religious significance, too. They are very special to the people who lent them for particular but different reasons, like special things belonging to you.

Committed to Judaism: A Jewish Community introduces you to ten Orthodox Jews who go to the United Synagogue in Hendon, North London. 'United Synagogue' is the name of a federation of synagogues founded in 1870. There are now forty-two member synagogues and twenty-four affiliated synagogues, between them serving thirty-eight thousand Jewish families in Britain. The United Synagogue also funds the Beth Din and a lot of the work of the Chief Rabbi.

SYLVIA AND BARRY SUTCLIFFE

ABOUT ME

NAME: *Amanda L*

WHAT I DO: *I go to a Jewish secondary school. I've opted to do French and German and Geography at GCSE as well as other subjects. We have lessons about Judaism, to learn about different aspects of it.*

SOME OF MY SPECIAL INTERESTS: *I like reading — anything, really. I'd like to do something with languages which involves travelling, perhaps working for a travel agency or a tour operator.*

MORE ABOUT ME

I've had my Bat Mitzvah. It wasn't that much of an ordeal. I gave a speech in shul and that's about it. But it's a pretty special occasion.

FACT-FINDER

Bat Mitzvah
Literally, 'Daughter of Commandments'. At the age of twelve, a Jewish girl reaches her religious maturity and becomes Bat Mitzvah. That is, she becomes responsible for performing the same Jewish religious commandments as an adult (e.g. fasting all day on Yom Kippur; see page 31).

Amanda is talking about the ceremony marking her becoming Bat Mitzvah. Her speech was a short explanation of that week's reading from the Torah (see page 19).

Shul
Pronounced *shool*, this is the Yiddish word (see opposite) for 'synagogue'.

NAME: *Leonie L*

WHAT I DO: *I go to a Jewish primary school. We do Jewish studies some of the time.*

SOME OF MY SPECIAL INTERESTS
I've got two fish: one goldfish and one koi carp.

NAME: *Jeffrey L*

WHAT I DO: *I work as a barrister.*

MY FAMILY: *I'm a Jewish parent with two daughters.*

MORE ABOUT ME

We live within easy walking distance of the synagogue. That's because the Torah forbids on the Sabbath what is called 'melachah' in Hebrew, usually translated as 'work'. A word like 'melachah', used four thousand years ago, doesn't translate very easily into English, so we have to keep a tradition of what it means. For example, getting on a bus and paying a fare doesn't sound like work but it does count as melachah.

My name is Jeffrey, but I also have the Hebrew name of Yom Tov. What happens is that, when Jewish babies are born or at the time of circumcision in the case of boys, we're given traditional Jewish names as well as secular ones. The Jewish name could be Hebrew or Yiddish or even Aramaic.

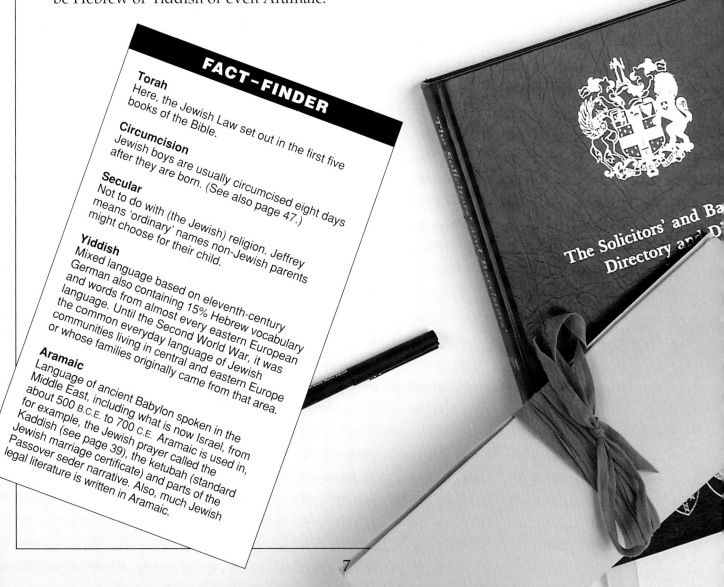

FACT-FINDER

Torah
Here, the Jewish Law set out in the first five books of the Bible.

Circumcision
Jewish boys are usually circumcised eight days after they are born. (See also page 47.)

Secular
Not to do with (the Jewish) religion. Jeffrey means 'ordinary' names non-Jewish parents might choose for their child.

Yiddish
Mixed language based on eleventh-century German also containing 15% Hebrew vocabulary and words from almost every eastern European language. Until the Second World War, it was the common everyday language of Jewish communities living in central and eastern Europe or whose families originally came from that area.

Aramaic
Language of ancient Babylon spoken in the Middle East, including what is now Israel, from about 500 B.C.E. to 700 C.E. Aramaic is used in, for example, the Jewish prayer called the Kaddish (see page 39), the ketubah (standard Jewish marriage certificate) and parts of the Passover seder narrative. Also, much Jewish legal literature is written in Aramaic.

The Solicitors' and Ba... Directory and D...

NAME: *Sandy L*

MY FAMILY: *I'm a New Yorker, part of a transatlantic family. I was brought up in an Orthodox community there quite like Hendon. There were many synagogues and most children went to Jewish day schools.*

My mother is English, my father American. My mother's family came to England from eastern Europe. My father's went to the United States from Latvia. I met Jeffrey through my grandparents in England.

WHAT I DO

I work as a food technologist in the Kashrut Division – that's the kosher-food section – of the Court of the Chief Rabbi. We investigate foods to find out if they're permissible according to Jewish dietary laws.

The Kashrut Division has a responsibility to the entire Jewish community in the United Kingdom. Our aim is to make it possible for people to choose kosher food wherever they happen to be shopping. Obviously, there's more certainty when you buy a product that's been made under rabbinic supervision – either our supervision or another supervising agency's. But that's not always possible. So we investigate commercially available foods and the results go into our *Really Jewish Food Guide*.

The Guide tells people whether a food is made under supervision or not. It tells them whether it's dairy, because we don't eat anything of dairy origin or with dairy ingredients in it with meat meals or after meat meals. The Guide also says whether the food is permitted or not. For example, in the confectionery listings some items are permitted, some are dairy, like Mars Bars, and some are not allowed at all because their ingredients aren't kosher.

We don't just list foodstuffs in the Guide. Cleaning-products that come into contact with food – on a plate, for instance – may not be kosher. Some washing-up liquids might use non-kosher animal-fats. So we list those as well.

I get information from the manufacturers to enable the rabbi in charge of the Kashrut Division to make a decision. It's not enough just to look at

the label and say the ingredients are OK. There are processing-agents, like anti-foams or stabilizers, to take into account. The food might share equipment with non-kosher items. For example, vegetarian baked beans manufactured on the same equipment as beans with sausages would be out of the question. Or the cans might go into a steam-oven at the same time as other cans to cook together. In certain circumstances, that wouldn't be permitted.

We also investigate medicines. Now if someone's life is in danger, not only may they but they must have any medication they need, whatever its source. The sanctity of human life comes first. In certain circumstances, you may break the Law to keep the Law. But with other aspects of medicine, there may be a choice between vitamin preparations, for instance, or between antibiotics or between taking a medicine in tablet or liquid form. Then we should opt for the kosher choice.

Keeping kosher isn't difficult. It's part of life. If someone were allergic to a particular food, they'd place importance on avoiding it. Jewish people are spiritually allergic, if you like, to certain ingredients. But we know what we like and we know what we can eat. It's a simple matter to double check on a list.

This year we're going to Brittany on holiday, so I've got a copy of the French Kashrut guide, the *Liste de Produits Cachers*, published by the central French Jewish organization. Normally, we choose a holiday destination with reference to the *Jewish Travel Guide*, which tells you where different Jewish facilities are. When we go to Brittany, we'll be taking meat with us and also our pots and pans and cutlery.

FACT-FINDER

Kashrut
The whole system of Jewish dietary laws.

Kosher
Permitted under Jewish Law.

Court of the Chief Rabbi
The Chief Rabbi (of Great Britain and the Commonwealth) is a learned man who has authority over a wide section of the Jewish community in Britain in matters of Jewish Law. Here, 'Court' is a translation of the Hebrew phrase 'Beth Din', literally 'House of the Law/Judgement'. This court makes rulings on matters of Jewish Law.

Rabbinic supervision
Supervision of a rabbi, who will have ensured that the product is kosher.

Sanctity
Sacredness.

Law
Sandy means Jewish Law.

Tourist Guide
MICHELIN
Brittany

NAME: *Eddie*

MY FAMILY: *I'm forty-nine. I was born in London into an Orthodox Jewish family.*

MY ROLE IN THE RELIGIOUS COMMUNITY

My father and his four brothers were some of the earliest members of this shul. So I've belonged to it since I was a boy and participated in all its activities. I went to a local Jewish school. It was only when I got married that I decided to leave, to have the experience of living in another Orthodox community. After five years, and with two small children, I came back.

I believe very much in community life, in family life and in the values that both of these help our children to develop. So I decided to take more responsibility in the life of the synagogue.

Initially, my main areas of interest were education and youth. I helped form the Hendon Kindergarten, now one of the most successful Jewish kindergartens in London. I was instrumental in setting up the Hendon Torah Centre for Jewish children aged twelve to eighteen. Children have the opportunity of going to Jewish primary schools until they are eleven, but many move on to non-Jewish secondary education. The Centre currently has seventy-five students who are continuing their studies at a high level.

Then about nine years ago I became an Honorary Officer of the synagogue. There's a Management Committee of thirty elected every year from a membership of about seventeen hundred people, and that Committee elects the Honorary Officers. For the first six years I was Treasurer, looking after the finances of what is a large but nevertheless aging and very mixed community – mixed in its religious commitment, mixed in age, mixed in motivation. We managed to remain solvent – just.

Since then, I've been Warden. This means I'm responsible for the general running of the synagogue but not the religious activities. I work with the Rabbi, the Chazzan, the Beadle, the synagogue secretaries and the Community Director.

A lot of people give a lot of their time to the community here. They may not share the same ideas or the same philosophy, but they back community initiatives. That's why we have a Community Director.

This is my last year as an Honorary Officer. I look back over a period which has been exciting for me and which has seen changes in the community which are important for the future of Jews in London. We think the community here is one that people will want to come and participate in.

FACT-FINDER

Shul
Pronounced *shool*, this is the Yiddish word (see page 7) for 'synagogue'.

Values
Ideas about what is right, what is wrong, what is of real value in life and how people should behave.

Kindergarten
Playschool or nursery school.

Torah
Here, Jewish teaching or instruction. (See also page 17.)

Rabbi
See page 13.

Chazzan
Cantor. A trained professional singer who chants the service and leads the congregation in prayer at the synagogue.

Beadle
The beadle (or 'shammas' in Hebrew) is generally an extremely knowledgeable person who acts as 'caretaker' of the religious side of running the synagogue. He sees to the smooth organization of the thrice-daily services, looks after the Torah scrolls, prayer-books, etc.

NAME: *Sidney*

WHAT I DO: *I'm the Rabbi at Hendon United Synagogue.*

MY FAMILY: *Isabelle and I have three children, a girl and two boys. They have all married and made aliyah, which means they've gone to live in Israel. We have ten grandchildren now, bless them. All Israeli born.*

SOME OF MY SPECIAL INTERESTS: *I am interested in sport and in art and I enjoy classical music. My first love was art. I won an art scholarship but didn't take it up. My art teacher was very angry at the time.*

I've brought an example of my work [see opposite]. It's a ketubah – a marriage certificate. The design, the artwork and the calligraphy are all my work. It's now being used throughout London. Apparently, there are now seven hundred and fifty to a thousand Jewish marriages a year in England.

MORE ABOUT ME

I was not particularly religious as a youngster, although I enjoyed going to the synagogue – I went with my grandfather. It was only when I was sixteen or seventeen years of age that I became interested in taking Judaism seriously. And I did. I went from Leeds, where I was born, to London and studied at Jews College, then part of London University. I was a BA in Hebrew and Aramaic and an MA. I then married, and about four years later I passed the rabbinical degree which gives me the title 'Rabbi'.

Hendon is the fifth position I have occupied as a rabbi. I started off as a youth minister in Hampstead Garden Suburb, looking after the young people of the community. I played sport with them. We had a Friday-evening study session together, and a Sabbath-morning youth service. Some of my pupils are now the leaders of the community there.

Then I moved to Ealing, from there to Newcastle upon Tyne, then to Bournemouth and finally Hendon. We've been in the Hendon community for twelve years now.

A community gets a rabbi by advertising in the Jewish press. The previous rabbi has left or sadly passed away or retired – usually retired. In fact, on three occasions I've arrived in my new community with the retired minister still coming to the synagogue.

What has given me a great thrill here in Hendon is that we now have on the synagogue campus six Sabbath services. There's the main service with a cantor, a choir and myself. There's an earlier service which takes the same form but without the cantor and choir. The congregation does its own thing and the prayers are read by lay people. About eighty attend that service. We have a youth service for youngsters from the age of thirteen up to about eighteen. They conduct their own service too. Some thirty young people attend.

There are two children's services, one for tiny tots up to the age of seven and another for children from seven up to the age of thirteen. These are taken by volunteer adults, young parents with their own youngsters. There's story-telling. They have a little Ark and a little Torah scroll that they take out. There's lots of singing and good fun.

We also have a service called the New Hendon Service for young people aged twenty to thirty-five. It has over two hundred and fifty young men and women attending regularly. Engagements are common, and that's the best thing which could happen. One of the rabbi's skills – and the rabbi's wife's skills – is trying to introduce people with a view to marriage. Somebody will ring me up seeking an introduction and I'll say, 'Have you been to the New Hendon Service? If not, why not? Come along. You'll meet someone there.' It happens. It's happening all the time.

We felt very proud when we won the Chief Rabbi's award for promoting our alternative services and for our wide range of activities – social, cultural and educational for young and old. There are forty different groups within the community.

FACT-FINDER

Aramaic
Language of ancient Babylon. Much Jewish legal literature is written in Aramaic. (See also page 7.)

Rabbi
Hebrew word meaning 'teacher'. To attain the rabbinic diploma requires years of study of Jewish teachings, particularly the Jewish Law, the Torah.

Cantor
Colleague of the rabbi. A cantor (or chazzan) is a trained professional singer who chants the service and leads the congregation in prayer at the synagogue.

Read by lay people
Sidney means the prayers are read by 'ordinary' members of the congregation, rather than being chanted by someone with special religious qualifications (e.g. a cantor or rabbi).

Ark • Torah scroll
The (main) Ark is the most sacred part of the synagogue because it is where the Torah scrolls are stored. Torah scrolls contain the first five books of the Bible (in Hebrew) and are carefully wrapped when not in use. They are always treated with great reverence. Jews read from a Torah scroll every Shabbat (Sabbath).

Chief Rabbi
The Chief Rabbi (of Great Britain and the Commonwealth) is a learned man who has authority over a wide section of the Jewish community in Britain in matters of Jewish Law.

TATE GALLERY
an illustrated companion

NAME: *Deborah N*

WHAT I DO: *I'm twenty-five. I studied architecture for my degree. Now I'm a Chartered Accountant, for my sins!*

SOME OF MY SPECIAL INTERESTS: *My interests are painting, eating and cinema. My husband's a doctor, which explains why we don't get to see as many films as I'd like to. I also like dancing, but in my present condition that's rather off the agenda. The baby's due in about three months.*

NAME: *Jeremy N*

WHAT I DO: *I'm a hospital doctor.*

SOME OF MY SPECIAL INTERESTS: *My interests are sport and music. I like jazz, classical, but I'm not too keen on the really contemporary pop. I play keyboard – piano – and compose a little bit.*

Sportswise, I'm playing cricket this afternoon. And, of course, I'm an armchair sportsman. I like golf.

I also like to mess about on the computer, play silly games.

That's about all I really get time for.

NAME: *Edna M*

WHAT I DO: *I'm in that glorious period of 'middle years'. I worked until fairly recently as a legal secretary.*

MY FAMILY: *We have two sons and two grandsons.*

MY ROLE IN THE RELIGIOUS COMMUNITY: *Both my husband and I come from religious homes, but there are many levels to that, of course. I like being involved with people. The synagogue is like an extension of our lives and we've always been very involved.*

SOME OF MY SPECIAL INTERESTS: *My other life is quite separate. We love music – classical music – and walking. We tend to walk even in towns and cities because that's the best way of seeing things. You see less, but what you do see you see in a more enlightening way, I think.*

NAME: *Louis M*

WHAT I DO: *I'm very happily retired, having reached my seventies. That means I can spend more time with my wife.*

When the War finished, I came out of the forces and started a metal-working business with my brothers. It's still going strong.

SOME OF MY SPECIAL INTERESTS: *Edna and I share our love of music and walking. And reading. We're both great readers. We belong to a delightful little book circle which meets in various people's houses. It's been going for nearly a hundred years. So, like Judaism itself, we feel duty bound to keep it going. I suppose it's my major interest outside the synagogue and home.*

FACT-FINDER

The War
Louis means the Second World War.

WHERE I BELONG

We're part of a long Jewish tradition which we feel very strongly. We're a close part of it. It's as relevant to us as it was to my great-grandparents, who kept it in Europe and died in the Holocaust. We feel that connection, but we're also modern people living at the end of the twentieth century. We try and live in a modern way which is also a good Jewish life.

Judaism is as diverse as the number of Jews there are. Every single person will do something that's different to somebody else. There's no one Jewish way. We do what suits us in the end. We set our own levels.

But when I tell people what I do, I sometimes feel like an exhibit. People ask, 'Do you really tape your fridge light on Shabbat?' I say, 'Yes, I do, because I don't want the light to come on. I don't cook. I don't use money....' All the don'ts make you sound like a strange creature. But what I do do is enjoy Shabbat. It's a day out of the twentieth century for a change. It's a day of rest, a day of relaxation. If people could know what that felt like, I think they'd understand exactly why we do it.

The bottom line is that everything you do feels right, so you find yourself doing more. No-one's saying 'You've got to do this' or 'You've got to do that'. I feel happy with what I do. I do it for myself. We do it for ourselves. It's a way of life.

DEBORAH N

FACT-FINDER

Holocaust
When millions of Jews were killed by the Nazis during the Second World War.

Shabbat
The Jewish Sabbath (see opposite).

Judaism is a way of life. It's not just praying when you are at the synagogue. You live it every day. When you eat, you bless God for the food. There's the administration of kashrut in the kitchen. That means keeping the milk and the meat separately, knowing the things you may buy and the things you may not, whether it's meat, fish, cheese, butter, sweets. Whatever it is, you have to be very careful to watch the ingredients, and make sure they are kosher.

We have in our Torah six hundred and thirteen commandments. Nobody can keep six hundred and thirteen commandments, the do's and the don'ts: two hundred and forty-eight positive commands and three hundred and sixty-five negative commands. But between us, the whole Jewish nation can keep the six hundred and thirteen commands.

According to many commentators, the six hundred and thirteen are really subdivisions of the Ten Commandments. Somehow, you find they're linked. So the Ten Commandments are the essence. You can't go away from the Ten Commandments. They teach us how to behave towards God and towards our fellow human beings. The commandments cover every moment of our lives.

Once Shabbat comes in, no work is permitted. Literally no more work. All the normal weekday things are finished with. We do not create on Shabbat. Even things like switching on a light or turning on the television are creative acts. By using a switch you create a circuit which produces light. So on Shabbat, the lights in the house work automatically on a time-switch. We do not answer the telephone. We do not watch television. If it's an act of creation we do not do it.

When I was young there weren't such things as time-switches. Once the Shabbat candles had burnt down or the fire in the grate had gone, we would either sit in the dark or go to bed. On Shabbat afternoon, we would sit as the evening darkened. The appearance of three stars signalled the end of Shabbat. Then we would switch on the lights and weekday 'work' would begin.

SIDNEY

FACT-FINDER

Kashrut • Kosher
'Kosher' means permitted under Jewish Law. Administering kashrut means keeping the whole system of Jewish dietary laws.

Torah • Ten Commandments
Here, 'Torah' means the first five books of the Bible. It includes the Ten Commandments (see Exodus 20:1–17).

Shabbat candles
Shabbat, the Jewish Sabbath, starts with the lighting of candles just before sunset on Friday.

The Jewish heritage is wonderfully satisfying. Our eldest son graduated from university here then went to Israel for six months. He stayed for two years and returned with an American fiancée. She's Jewish. They're now married with two small children.

My great delight is that they bring up the children in a very traditional way. So, when they're in our home or we're in theirs, which is three thousand miles away, Friday night is the same. The candles are lit. The challot, the bread, is blessed. They recite the Kiddush, the blessing over the wine, in the same way that we do. They go to the services on Shabbat with us here or in Boston. It's very gratifying.

I'm aware more than ever in these days that your children are only yours for a short time. When they're little, you try to give them a sense of values and pass on to them what you believe to be right. It may seem hard at the time, but as you get older you find out that that's the easy bit. The hard part is learning to accept what they do with what you and others have taught them. They do adapt things. They do live differently. But the fact that my sons retain their Jewishness is gratifying.

EDNA M

FACT-FINDER

Shabbat
The Jewish Sabbath, which starts on Friday evening. These services are on Saturday.

Values
Edna means a sense of what is right, what is wrong, what is of real value in life and how people should behave.

I feel I belong in the synagogue. Our strict religious duties can be performed anywhere. But it's desirable to pray certain types of prayer with a minimum of ten people and in suitable surroundings.

A synagogue is a place where you go to pray. It's holy whilst it's being used as a synagogue. All over Britain, you'll see buildings originally used for some other purpose which became consecrated as synagogues when a Jewish community grew up there. If the Jews have moved on – which happens, because we're a very mobile people – then the religious items are removed and the building is deconsecrated. It's just another pile of stones.

JEFFREY L

I can pray at home – I don't need to go to the synagogue. So my life is far more my own to live than my husband's in that respect. Women are obliged to pray, they just don't have to leave the home to do it.

When we go on holiday, we take the prayer-books and the Torah and we're portable. I can still perform the commandments. On a Friday night, it's the lighting of the candles, not what they're stuck into, that matters. It's having the loaves of bread on the table, not what covers them or is underneath them, that matters. It's not the objects that are important, it's the action.

So to go on holiday and see the same candles, the same bread, the same wine but pared down to the essentials, it focuses the mind. To create something beautiful out of very basic objects is very satisfying.

SANDY L

FACT-FINDER

Consecrated
Made sacred, or holy.

Torah
Here, a book containing the first five 'books' of the Bible. Each year, Jews read the entire Torah. There is a set section read each week by Jews the world over. Sandy and her family take the Torah so that they can keep up with those readings.

Commandments
Sandy means she can still keep the Jewish Law, including keeping Shabbat (the Sabbath).

19

I came more to observing the Jewish way of life in my teens. I suppose it started in a social context. My parents wanted to make sure they had a son who didn't marry out – the bottom line for most Orthodox but non-observant middle–class Jewish families. So they sent me off to a Jewish youth group. I just felt really comfortable there.

People talk about the Jewish soul having a spark in it, a spark which is passed down. I believe I have that spark in me. Just mixing in those circles and slowly learning more about Jewish traditions and beliefs, I got more and more into it.

You reach a spiritual level, then you try to push it a bit, move it on a bit at a time. It's a dynamic thing. There are times when something that was easy last week is really difficult this week. That's all part of the challenge.

JEREMY N

FACT–FINDER

Marry out
Marry someone who wasn't a Jew.

Non-observant
Jeremy means families who no longer follow most of the Orthodox Jewish rules for daily life. For example, families who do not keep kosher and/or do not keep Shabbat (the Sabbath).

WHAT I FEEL STRONGLY ABOUT

One of the things I feel strongest about is people. Not being judgemental about people, which is sometimes hard. I mean approaching life as a reasonable human being.

I've never had any tremendously high goals. I married young, so I haven't had much time to sit back and think about what I'd like to do. It's all sort of happened. But when a worthwhile project comes along, I give it everything I've got. I don't take on anything I can't fulfil.

EDNA M

Judaism isn't to be judged by what Jews do or how they behave. Judaism is the Torah, the writings around it. It's how Jews should try to behave. It's about ideals and concepts which I personally feel are for ever, which don't change with time. They're as relevant today as they'll be in another five thousand years.

JEREMY N

FACT-FINDER

Torah
Here, the Jewish Law set out in the first five books of the Bible.

As a Jew in Britain at the end of the twentieth century, the life I lead is the result of thousands of years of history and also of the last hundred years of history. I know what lies behind where I am now. I have the tradition of a particular relationship with God, with his purpose on earth and what he wants me to do. But in this day and age, that takes a certain amount of effort and concentration. It may be that the last hundred years turn out to be more important to Jewish life than the thousands.

A hundred years ago, my grandfather emigrated from western Russia, where there was a large Jewish population. The place where he lived must have been a Jewish town with a strong spiritual life. But standards of living were low there. Jews were continually being attacked by the communities living around them, whipped up to strong anti-Jewish fervour. Killings of Jewish people systematically took place in what were called pogroms. So, in about 1890, along with hundreds of thousands of other Jews, he emigrated to Britain, to Aberdeen.

He brought with him strong spiritual values and an automatic, unquestioning Jewish background. My father's generation, born over here, had quite different opportunities. They grew up surrounded by the materialistic values of a developed country. Many drifted away from commitment to a Jewish life. They married and raised children who are even further from the kind of life my grandfather knew as a child. The world of Jewish children today is one where they're confronted all the time by values reflecting material gain or quick and easy pleasure or satisfaction.

I have to say that, when I was a young man, I wasn't particularly committed to a Jewish religious life. It took getting married and having children to make us think about the sort of family we wanted and the background we wanted it to have. Since then, we've gradually got closer to a traditionally religious Jewish way of life.

I think the number of people you can now call Jews has dropped. There's a big difference between being Jewish in a deep, interior sense and being Jewish just because you can say you have Jewish ancestors.

Being Jewish means being involved in Jewish religious life: fulfilling our side of the Covenant entered into between God and our ancestors. What was agreed then applies to us now.

Everybody knows there was a time – I was born during it – when Nazi armies under Hitler were trying to kill every Jew. They didn't succeed. But if we, the surviving Jews, don't continue to be Jewish, in another hundred years we'll have completed Hitler's work. There won't be any Jews.

JEFFREY L

FACT-FINDER

Materialistic values
Belief that material things are more important than anything else.

Our side of the Covenant
The Jews' side of the agreement between God and Abraham later renewed through Moses. That is, keeping God's Law as set out in the Torah, the first five books of the Bible. (See also page 47.)

I feel strongly about the way the Arab countries which surround Israel are always attacking Israel. Apart from anything else, it seems like they're making a big fuss over a little piece of land. The other countries are much bigger than Israel.

AMANDA L

England is my interest, my great interest. If I feel strongly about anything it's the damage that's been done to England. This is our country. We're Jewish. We have a great belief in the future of the Jewish people in Israel. But in the meantime, England is the country I live in.

I've seen it destroyed. Ribbon building started in my childhood. I saw the fields of Middlesex being devoured. Beautiful old villages have been shaken to pieces by through traffic. Then there's so much bad architecture. I feel there's very little to be done now. Conservation – that was an unheard-of word – has such an uphill fight on its hands.

LOUIS M

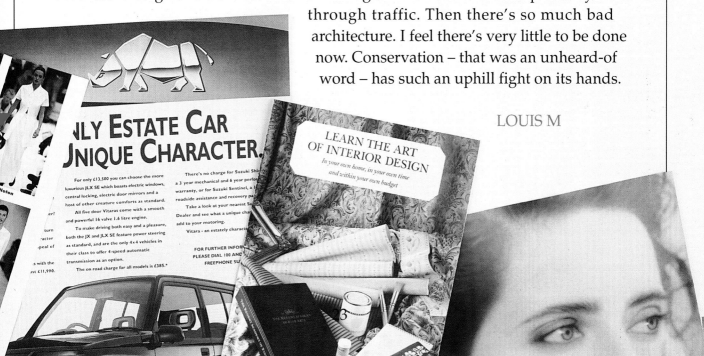

NLY ESTATE CAR
JNIQUE CHARACTER.

For only £13,500 you can choose the more luxurious JLX SE which boasts electric windows, central locking, electric door mirrors and a host of other creature comforts as standard.

All five door Vitaras come with a smooth and powerful 16 valve 1.6 litre engine.

To make driving both easy and a pleasure, both the JX and JLX SE feature power steering as standard, and are the only 4x4 vehicles in their class to offer 4-speed automatic transmission as an option.

The on road charge for all models is £385.*

There's no charge for Suzuki Shi... a 3 year mechanical and 8 year perfor... warranty, or for Suzuki Sentinel, a ... roadside assistance and recovery pa...

Take a look at your nearest Su... Dealer and see what a unique char... add to your motoring.

Vitara - an estately charact...

FOR FURTHER INFOR...
PLEASE DIAL 100 AND ...
FREEPHONE SU...

LEARN THE ART OF INTERIOR DESIGN
In your own home, in your own time and within your own budget

I'm very frightened by the decline of Orthodox Judaism. The only area of increase in Anglo-Jewry is on the 'far right', amongst extremely Orthodox Jews. The middle, centrist Judaism, is declining. The United Synagogue in particular is declining. It's regarded as antiquated. Its people come across as boring.

My son is a boy of twenty-two. When he left school he went to Israel, to a yeshivah, which is a seminary for advanced Jewish studies. He then volunteered to serve in the Israeli army in a special scheme for yeshivah students. He served in a combat unit during the Gulf War. He has said, as a young Jewish man, that he would not want to live in London and participate in centrist Judaism here because it's not committed. It's all over the place. To an extent my daughter, who's two years younger, shares this view.

In my view, the very committed young people we need here are going. They're either leaving centrist Judaism or they're going to Israel. The people who are left are less involved in activities which show a commitment to Orthodox Judaism.

Take the example of a cousin of mine. He married a less Orthodox wife and now leads a less Orthodox lifestyle. Their son recently married into an even less Orthodox family. At his wedding we didn't even feel we were Jewish. I'm concerned that the only contact his children will have with anything Jewish is at Yom Kippur.

This is something that's happened in my own family in the space of just twenty-five years. I'm sure it could be multiplied any number of times. I think there's an erosion of commitment.

EDDIE

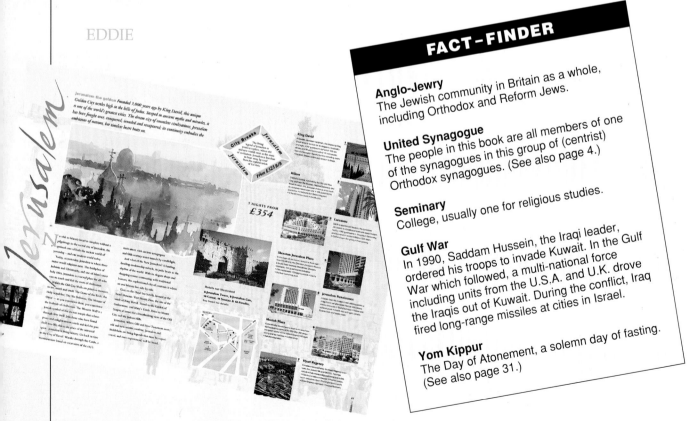

FACT-FINDER

Anglo-Jewry
The Jewish community in Britain as a whole, including Orthodox and Reform Jews.

United Synagogue
The people in this book are all members of one of the synagogues in this group of (centrist) Orthodox synagogues. (See also page 4.)

Seminary
College, usually one for religious studies.

Gulf War
In 1990, Saddam Hussein, the Iraqi leader, ordered his troops to invade Kuwait. In the Gulf War which followed, a multi-national force including units from the U.S.A. and U.K. drove the Iraqis out of Kuwait. During the conflict, Iraq fired long-range missiles at cities in Israel.

Yom Kippur
The Day of Atonement, a solemn day of fasting. (See also page 31.)

I was listening to a tape of my children singing earlier. They were singing a prayer. The first words translate into English as 'I believe with a perfect faith'. It's said that when the Jews were taken to the gas-chambers they went singing that prayer.

LATEST CEASEFIRE FARCE

'I believe with a perfect faith ...' is one of the Thirteen Principles laid down by Maimonides: 'I believe with a perfect faith that the Messiah is coming.'

We do not say that the Messiah has come. If you look at the world, how can he have come? That is why Jews do not accept any person or any being or any belief which says that we have already seen the Messiah. The world has not been put to rights. According to our belief, when the Messiah comes the world will be a paradise. People will live at peace with each other. There will be tolerance – between the strong and the weak, black and white, Jew, Christian and Muslim. There will be no more war. Swords will be turned into plough-shares, spears into pruning-hooks. And the lion will lie down with the lamb. Those Messianic visions of a beautiful world have yet to be turned into reality.

But we believe that the Messiah will come. As a result of all the persecution we have been through, the Jews of all peoples have more reason to say that he will never come. But we repeat it over and over again: 'I believe with a perfect faith.' We believe that it's going to happen. The Messiah will come – the Jew is the eternal optimist.

So that is a very, very deep and basic belief. It gives us, I think, an attitude to life that, in spite of what we have been through, we must still smile and get on with life. We should not be downhearted in our personal difficulties. The darkest clouds have a silver lining.

SIDNEY

FACT-FINDER

Gas-chambers
Where hundreds of thousands of Jews died in Nazi concentration camps during the Second World War.

Thirteen Principles • Maimonides
Moses Maimonides (1135–1204), born in Cordoba in Spain, was a rabbi and perhaps the most famous and most important Jewish thinker and scholar of all time. His codes of law are the basis of the Jewish legal system. He also composed Thirteen Principles of Jewish faith by which Jews must live.

Messiah
Hebrew title meaning 'God's anointed one'. (The title 'Christ' comes from a Greek word meaning 'anointed one'.)

Messianic visions
You can find descriptions of what Jews believe will happen when the Messiah comes, i.e. Messianic visions, in the Bible. See, e.g., Micah 4:1–5 and Isaiah 2:2–4 or 11:1–9.

MY FAVOURITE FESTIVAL

P esach is my favourite festival. It's got a lot of historical significance. With Pesach, I can see a link between the present and the past more than with the other festivals. I can see the reason for what we do.

I like the whole thing. I especially like the songs at the end. They're in praise of God. We all sing together.

AMANDA L

I particularly enjoy and get a lot out of Pesach. It commemorates the time when our ancestors left slavery in Egypt. They were taken out on the firm promise that they were going to be a special people performing God's will in a special place. They were going to use their freedom for a specific religious purpose. We celebrate that, with all its religious associations.

I was brought up in a home where Pesach was celebrated traditionally. That means there are lots of detailed bits of observance. You don't just buy a box of matzos and stick it on the table and that's Pesach. It doesn't happen like that. But some Jews have drifted, generation by generation, with less and less knowledge about Judaism. Among them, it could get to the point where a box of matzos is stuck on the table. Then their grandchildren may have values so very different that you don't even get a box of matzos.

JEFFREY L

FACT-FINDER

Pesach
Passover.

Bits of observance
Actions that should be performed.

Matzos
Jeffrey means a special type of large biscuit made from plain flour and water only, always under rabbinic supervision (see pages 8 and 9) for Passover. At the Passover meal, matzos represent the unleavened bread (i.e. bread baked without anything that would make it rise, such as yeast) eaten by the Israelites at the first Passover.

Values
Here, ideas about what is important.

I love Sukkoth because of building the sukkahs and the earthiness of it, but the most significant festival to me is Pesach. It's the celebration of freedom.

Freedom's the theme that runs through everything we should be thinking of all the time. We're supposed to remember day and night that God brought us out of Egypt. What runs through everything and influences how we should behave in our lives is the thought that we were once slaves. Associated with that is Moses receiving the Torah. So it's a very important time.

Then there's the seder night. It's a big family gathering. Can be stressful, but it's very nice.

JEREMY N

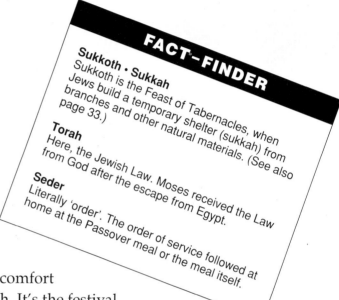

FACT-FINDER

Sukkoth • Sukkah
Sukkoth is the Feast of Tabernacles, when Jews build a temporary shelter (sukkah) from branches and other natural materials. (See also page 33.)

Torah
Here, the Jewish Law. Moses received the Law from God after the escape from Egypt.

Seder
Literally 'order'. The order of service followed at home at the Passover meal or the meal itself.

The festival that gives me greatest comfort from every point of view is Pesach. It's the festival of freedom. It's a family time. It's easily understandable to people like me. I feel part of what happened in this freedom.

That's why, in two years' time, when my two children have finished at university here, my family and I are going to live in Israel. There you're completely free as a Jew to live in whichever way you wish. For example, walking in the street wearing a skull-cap. My son does that here. I don't. He can defend himself if someone throws a bottle at him. I don't feel I'd be able to.

I want to be free to practise my religion and to live a Jewish life. So Pesach, for me, is an important festival.

EDDIE

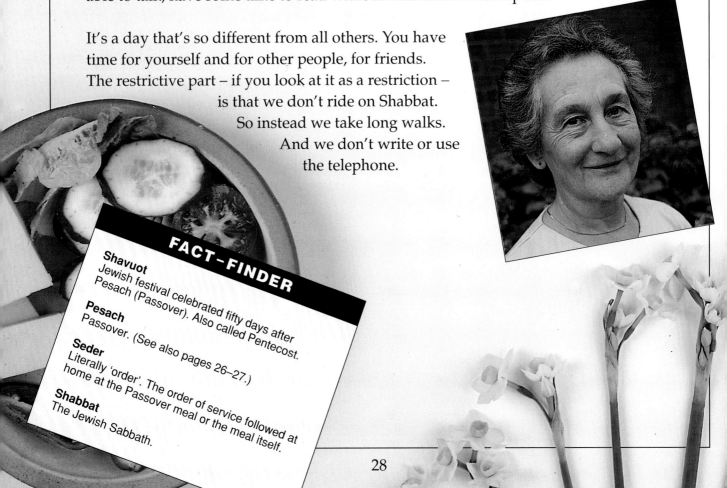

All the festivals are wonderful occasions. They provide a discipline to life which brings family togetherness, right from childhood, and that's wonderful.

I think, if there is a favourite or a most significant one, it's Shavuot. For several reasons. Firstly, it comes in the spring. It's the time of the giving of the Law to Moses which is, after all, the foundation of everything. Secondly, it's just two days. They're two fairly relaxed days when traditionally we have a milk diet – meat is not normally eaten at that time. The synagogues are decorated with flowers. There's a very light, uplifting and religious feeling. For me, it's perhaps the nicest time.

Pesach is also wonderful because it tells the marvellous story of how the Jews came out of Egypt. You can tell that story in so many different colours and shades that it's always delightful. It makes a great coming-togetherness of families. You usually invite friends and perhaps people who wouldn't normally take part in a seder. But the effort, the work done preparing for Pesach, is still very hard on the woman, even with modern aids. It's tough, but we enjoy it. It's wonderfully satisfying when you get there.

Although it's not a festival as such, Shabbat is wonderful, too. I think our children at one time felt it was rather restrictive, but we tried not to make it so. After a hard working week, it's always a pleasure to come together, relax, eat a meal together, be able to talk, have some time to read without humdrum interruption.

It's a day that's so different from all others. You have time for yourself and for other people, for friends. The restrictive part – if you look at it as a restriction – is that we don't ride on Shabbat. So instead we take long walks. And we don't write or use the telephone.

FACT-FINDER

Shavuot
Jewish festival celebrated fifty days after Pesach (Passover). Also called Pentecost.

Pesach
Passover. (See also pages 26–27.)

Seder
Literally 'order'. The order of service followed at home at the Passover meal or the meal itself.

Shabbat
The Jewish Sabbath.

28

I remember the children sometimes fighting it. One of my sons was particularly challenging, and it made me think long and hard. You grow into a discipline, a whole way of life. Once you've accepted it, it's very difficult to explain to someone else why, for instance, you hold back from doing this or that. Even now, I sometimes have problems with the details of do's and don'ts. I think what matters more is that you stick to the basics of the religion while living a full life. Sometimes that's complicated, but as I get older I find it easier to accept.

EDNA M

My favourite festival's Shavuot, though not for the same reasons as Edna. It's because Shavuot comes at the end of a long period of mourning following Pesach. I've always thought it's rather a dreary period. There are forty-eight days of mourning and one day in between as an exception. Most of the recorded tragedies from our past have happened in that period, and this is when we mourn them. It doesn't cover recent history, of course. If it did, we'd be mourning three hundred and sixty-five days of the year.

So at the end of this period of mourning, Shavuot is a very happy occasion. It's short and sweet and very colourful. It's a happy time, one I like a lot.

And there's Pesach. I always think of that play 'Dear Octopus', by Dodie Smith, about a family getting together at Christmas. It's about the tentacles of family life reaching out and pulling everyone together, in spite of the pressures – past and present – that every family has. That covers our experience, too, at Pesach.

LOUIS M

For this rabbi, every festival has an excitement and it also has an anxiety. I have to get through the festival. I have to think of a message and present it to the congregation, perform in the synagogue, read the Law, sing, speak. The festivals are always tense for me. I begin to breathe with relief when a festival is coming to a conclusion.

For the festival of Shavuot, some stay up all night in order to study. I'll stay up part of the night and get up early to go back to the synagogue. The ones who stay up all night have a service among themselves very early in the morning then go home to bed to sleep it off. By then, the rest of the congregation is starting to get up and come into synagogue. So I have to stay up late and get up early to be with the main congregation.

Yom Kippur is a strain because you're fasting and you have to speak and take part in the service with no food or drink. But the festival where there's a lot of hard physical work is Sukkoth. We have to put up the sukkah. We have a lovely sukkah here at home which seats nine or ten people and stands on the patio. Guests come during the festival. Youngsters come. We have in Hendon what's called a 'sukkah crawl'. The kids go from one sukkah to another. At each house they get something to eat and drink. They sit and make a blessing over the food. They also keep a chart and give marks to decide whose sukkah's the best.

Pesach is a very happy festival and again the preparation is very hard work. There is a lot of pressure at home. For Pesach, we clean the house from top to bottom. Every cupboard is cleaned – not a crumb left behind. The books come out to be cleaned. In the kitchen, all the pots and pans, crockery, cutlery, every single item is changed. Meaty and milky crockery and cutlery and all the cooking utensils for Pesach are separate. During the year we eat bread daily. On Pesach normal (leavened) bread is forbidden. All our utensils are therefore changed because of their contact with bread.

But that first seder night of Pesach is a good time. We have a full table of family and guests. This year, please God, we'll have our daughter and son-in-law and their three boys, and our son and daughter-in-law might come from Israel with their four little ones. That is our reward, when all the family celebrate the festival together, and Pesach is *the* family festival.

SIDNEY

FACT-FINDER

Read the Law
Sidney means that he has to read from the Torah, the first five books of the Bible.

Shavuot
Festival, also called the Feast of Weeks or Pentecost, held fifty days after Pesach (Passover). It commemorates the giving of the Ten Commandments by God to Moses. (See also pages 28–29.)

Yom Kippur
The Day of Atonement, the most sacred day in the Jewish calendar. Jews neither eat nor drink for twenty-five hours and there is a day-long service in the synagogue.

Sukkoth · Sukkah
Sukkoth is the Feast of Tabernacles, when Jews build a temporary shelter (sukkah) from branches and other natural materials. (See also page 33.)

Pesach
Passover. (See also pages 26–27.)

Meaty and milky
Jewish food laws do not allow meat and dairy ingredients to be cooked together or eaten at the same meal. Jews who keep kosher therefore use separate sets of crockery, etc., for all 'meaty' and 'milky' food.

Seder
Literally 'order'. The order of service followed at home at the Passover meal or the meal itself.

Rosh Hashanah
Jewish New Year festival, celebrated in September/October. The first ten days of the new year are a special time for repentance (being sorry for wrong-doing). Yom Kippur (the tenth day) ends the festival.

I like Rosh Hashanah. It's the start of another new year. It's a fresh start and you feel like you're holier.

We eat bread and honey and apple and honey. The honey's for a sweet year. There's round loaves of bread. That's because the year goes round.

We blow a ram's horn, a shofar. I can't get a single note out of it. The shofar gets blown a hundred times, including once on Yom Kippur. There are notes of different lengths – like three short notes or nine very short notes. They've all got names.

LEONIE L

I t's very difficult to say which festival is a favourite, but I think it's probably Sukkoth. It's a lovely time. You've had Rosh Hashanah and you've survived Yom Kippur.

I say 'survived' because Yom Kippur is very hard. I find fasting very hard, and we fast for twenty-five hours. Also, you're trying to reach a sort of spiritual level in an atmosphere that sometimes makes it difficult to concentrate. People talk. There's a lot of noise. It's hard to find significance in some of the prayers. Jeremy, my husband, puts his tallith over his head and tries to ignore what's going on around him.

Sukkoth is almost a harvest festival, but it's more than that. It really makes you feel close to the Israelites and the way they lived, close to nature, close to the elements. In this country in September/October that's certainly something you notice.

We build the sukkahs, the booths, outside and we sit outside. Some people sleep in them overnight, although I haven't done that personally.

We don't sit in them in all weather. If it rains, we don't have to. But it's a very practical and a very real experience. You're not in a synagogue. Everyone can participate. What's interesting is that, although women aren't commanded to sit in the sukkah as men are, they've taken it on themselves as one of the things they do. Sometimes I'll be told I can sit under a particular part of the sukkah although it isn't kosher and it won't matter to me. So I say, 'If I'm going to sit here in the cold, it's going to matter.'

We don't have a sukkah of our own because we live in a flat. So we share our friends' sukkah, which is very nice. People decorate their sukkahs in really gorgeous ways. You have leaves on top and fruit and vegetables dangling down. It can be literally any sort – onions, apples, pomegranates. They're in little string bags. Our friends have chillies dangling down, strategically placed over their father's head. Other decorations are put up – children's drawings, pictures from Israel. It's always very bright.

The combination of that and sitting out there in October when 'normal' people are inside – I love it. I really enjoy it.

DEBORAH N

Sukkoth is my favourite festival. It's long, it's relaxed and there's no mad rush at the end to pack it all away.

With Pesach, for instance, there's a deadline for getting ready, for doing the cleaning and getting everything out. That's fine. But at the end of Pesach, there's a complete reverse upheaval. You have to put all the Pesach dishes away again, get everything tidied up, bring out the year-round stuff. So Pesach ends in chaos.

Sukkoth doesn't. We've got the high holy days behind us. Yom Kippur, which looms large, is over. Sukkoth is a time for sitting, and enjoying friends and community, and the weather – if it's good, it's good, if it isn't, it isn't. You have the chance to ease into Sukkoth then ease out of it. It's long enough to enjoy.

SANDY L

FACT-FINDER

Sukkoth
Literally, tabernacles, booths or shelters (singular: sukkah). Sukkoth, the Feast of Tabernacles, starts four days after Yom Kippur and lasts for seven days. At Sukkoth, Jews remember how the Israelites lived in temporary shelters in the desert after their escape from Egypt. The rules about celebrating Sukkoth are set out in the Torah (see, e.g., Leviticus 23:42–43 in the Bible).

Rosh Hashanah • Yom Kippur
Rosh Hashanah (Jewish New Year) is celebrated in September/October. The first ten days of the new year are a special time for repentance (being sorry for wrong-doing). The tenth day is Yom Kippur (Day of Atonement), the most sacred day in the Jewish calendar. Jews neither eat nor drink for twenty-five hours and there is a day-long service in the synagogue.

Tallith
Prayer-shawl used by Jewish men.

Kosher
Permitted under Jewish Law.

Pesach
Passover. (See also pages 26–27 and 30.)

A SPECIAL MOMENT

C oming out of the Army at the end of the War was a special moment. I fought in North Africa and in Italy. I was in Italy when Italy surrendered. We'd seen such a lot of action that I never thought I'd see home again. I thought, if I come out of this, I'll be a very lucky man indeed. And I managed it. Those were very momentous days.

The State of Israel Declaration Day was also special. I thought that would be the end of Jewish troubles. I thought we could exist alongside the Arabs very easily. I thought the Semitic peoples would recognize each other's needs, wants and privileges. But nothing comes easily in politics.

LOUIS M

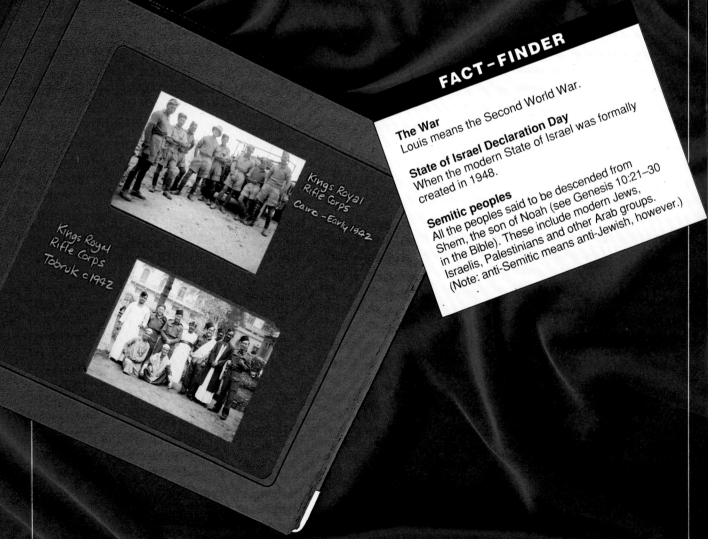

Kings Royal Rifle Corps
Cairo - Early 1942

Kings Royal Rifle Corps
Tobruk c 1942

FACT-FINDER

The War
Louis means the Second World War.

State of Israel Declaration Day
When the modern State of Israel was formally created in 1948.

Semitic peoples
All the peoples said to be descended from Shem, the son of Noah (see Genesis 10:21–30 in the Bible). These include modern Jews, Israelis, Palestinians and other Arab groups. (Note: anti-Semitic means anti-Jewish, however.)

W hat moved me most was something extremely simple. At the age of twenty I was travelling to Israel for the first time, by boat. Suddenly, out of the mist on the horizon, Mount Carmel appeared. I don't think anything can quite recapture that moment. This was my first sight of the country that came with the promise that came with the Covenant made so many thousands of years ago.

JEFFREY L

FACT-FINDER

Mount Carmel
Mountain near the port of Haifa. Scene of a dramatic contest between the prophet Elijah and the priests of Baal (see 1 Kings 18:17–40 in the Bible).

Promise ... Covenant
Jeffrey means God's promise to Abraham and later to Moses that his people (i.e. the Jews) would have a land of their own if they kept God's Laws. (See also page 47.)

Candle-lighting time
Sandy means when she (as wife and mother of the family) lights the Shabbat (Sabbath) candles just before sunset every Friday evening. Shabbat begins the moment after the candles are lit (since creating a flame is forbidden on Shabbat).

I f I were to pick a special moment I would say it's that second at candle-lighting time every week when everything stops. Things that have had to be done are either done or put away, and that's it. The week's over. There's nothing that calls me. Not the washing that still needs doing or a letter to write or a bill to be paid or a television programme. Nothing.

It's that moment when everything stops and an incredible peace descends. It's like calling time-out in the hectic pace of life. I work hard for it, very hard. But I get that special moment every week, and I really like it.

SANDY L

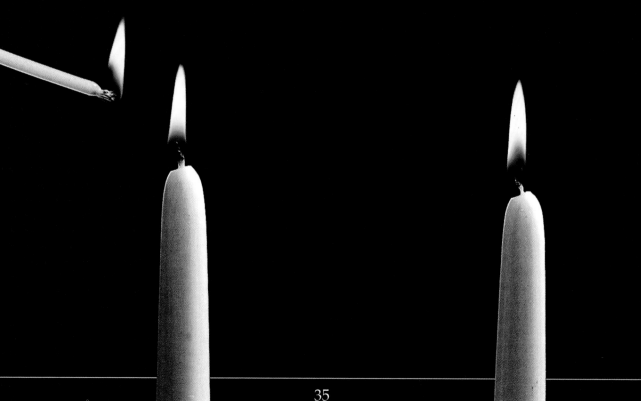

Our wedding is our special moment. We got married here in this synagogue in July 1990. There was a particularly loving feeling about it.

The wedding is a very short service. There's something quite intense being there under the chuppah, the canopy. Although there are lots of people about, it's very intimate. You've got your parents with you. We had beautiful music – clarinet – which was very haunting. The whole thing happens very quickly.

Then, after it was over, the place went mad. Our friends danced us out from the chuppah. It was very exciting. There was a lovely atmosphere. At the party afterwards there was a lot of Israeli dancing – with a skipping-rope, a big parasol with ribbons, that sort of thing. It's traditional to entertain the bride and groom after their wedding, so people do dances and silly things like juggling in front of you.

It was a very special day: a really family-centred event. There was a great feeling between our two families. This is very important to us, because we feel that family is so important.

DEBORAH N

The biggest, most important, most wonderful moment in my life was the birth of my first child. Without question. Having a faith, you do think about the future and wanting to do the right thing for the future. If you've created your own morsel of the future, it does strengthen your sense of commitment.

EDNA M

G etting married, to me, was the most important thing in my life. Raising a Jewish family, an observant Jewish family, is what I feel my purpose here is. So you feel very much a sense of tradition under the chuppah. It's something which has come down through thousands of years, like the ceremony itself. It's quite a nerve-wracking moment, but extremely exciting.

When you're danced out by your friends, it's marvellous. You feel it's a communal thing, the whole wedding. People are coming to your wedding, being happy at your wedding, enjoying it. That's a wonderful feeling. It's a celebration of us.

What makes marriage significant is its role in continuity. We're commanded – Jewish men are commanded – to be fruitful and multiply. That's actually the first positive commandment in the Torah. Opinions differ, but this is often interpreted as meaning having at least one male and one female child. So part of the significance of marriage is that you're fulfilling one of God's commandments.

FACT-FINDER

Observant Jewish family
One which keeps the Jewish Law and takes an active part in Jewish religious life.

Chuppah
Wedding canopy; see opposite. (The photographs above show a parasol, not the chuppah.)

Torah
Here, the Jewish Law set out in the first five books of the Bible.

Also, I want to pass on to my children everything that I enjoy about my religion. I'm very aware of our recent history, the last fifty years or so. I feel very strongly about raising a family with a strong Jewish identity. Trying to recoup our losses, if you like.

JEREMY N

A special moment for me was when I met my wife. We were at a Hebrew seminar together. The seminar was in Switzerland. I met Isabelle by the lake, Lac Léman. It was very romantic. And, of course, it was very significant. That moment changed my life for ever. We have been married now thirty-six years.

SIDNEY

WORDS THAT MEAN A LOT TO ME

We've been described as the People of the Book, but really we're the people of books. If you lead a Jewish life, you spend a lot of time not just reading the Torah but reading and discussing commentaries on the Torah. Also what rabbis have said about those commentaries down through the ages.

This book I've brought to show you is by Al-Sheikh. He was writing in Turkey and northern Israel in about 1500. What makes it special is its history.

My father rescued it from burial. Jewish people don't burn their books. Other people burn our books. We revere books. Books with God's name in them are particularly special. We mustn't destroy anything with God's name in it. When books containing God's name get too tattered or decrepit to be put to their proper use, they're buried with someone at a funeral. It's a mark of honour for a person to be buried in this way.

This book, which has got God's name all over it, was sent for burial. My father, who worked as a Jewish-cemetery superintendent, noticed it was only its binding that was damaged. The book itself was good, and you don't bury books that are good.

It was printed in Amsterdam in 1780. I imagine it would have been brought to England by a family rather like my grandfather's. They'd gathered up their most precious possessions, and Al-Sheikh's commentary was one of them.

JEFFREY L

FACT-FINDER

People of the Book
Here, 'the Book' is the (Jewish) Bible.

Torah
Here, the first five books of the Bible, which contain the Jewish Law.

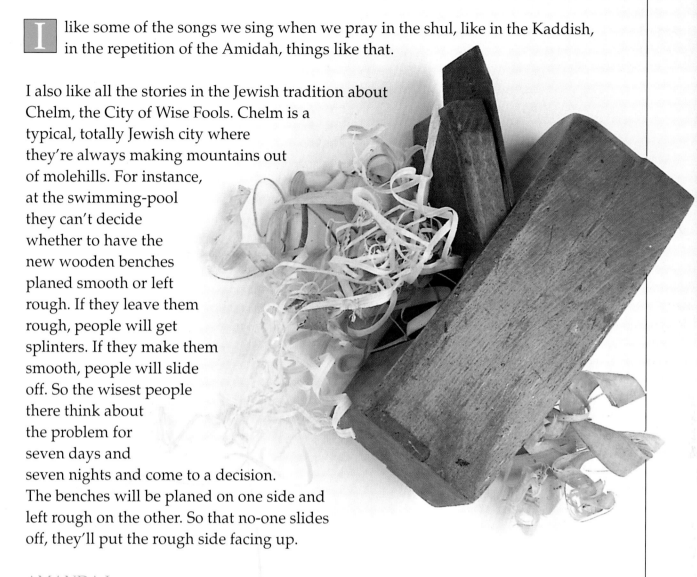

I like some of the songs we sing when we pray in the shul, like in the Kaddish, in the repetition of the Amidah, things like that.

I also like all the stories in the Jewish tradition about Chelm, the City of Wise Fools. Chelm is a typical, totally Jewish city where they're always making mountains out of molehills. For instance, at the swimming-pool they can't decide whether to have the new wooden benches planed smooth or left rough. If they leave them rough, people will get splinters. If they make them smooth, people will slide off. So the wisest people there think about the problem for seven days and seven nights and come to a decision. The benches will be planed on one side and left rough on the other. So that no-one slides off, they'll put the rough side facing up.

AMANDA L

I like the books about Savta Simcha. The words mean Grandmother Joy. She lives in a house in Jerusalem and goes travelling around and meets a whole load of children and they become her family. She has adventures with them. She carries a big samovar around and she's got a big bag. She calls it her Shabbat bag and it's got everything in it.

LEONIE L

FACT-FINDER

Shul
Pronounced *shool*, this is the Yiddish word (see page 7) for 'synagogue'.

Kaddish
Literally 'holiness'. A prayer praising God said or chanted at key points in prayers when a minyan (see page 42) is present. It is the most significant and sacred and one of the most ancient of all Jewish prayers. It is also recited by those mourning a close relative.

Amidah
Literally 'standing'. Central prayer of the Jewish faith, so named because worshippers stand when they recite it and face Jerusalem.

Samovar
Russian word meaning a type of hot-water urn used for making tea in eastern Europe and Asia.

Shabbat
The Jewish Sabbath.

My favourite words are probably modern Hebrew, even though I don't have an excellent command of it.

I think it's one of the ways we're close to Israel. I think it's very important for young Jewish people to feel that connection and learn the language, which is a living language. It feels like our language.

I think we feel a fairly close connection to Israel. We've both been there. We've got a lot of friends who've gone to live there. It's our hope that we will go to live in Israel with our family. The continuity of Jewish family life means that if we don't get there, our children will.

No, we will go. It's not that we in any way don't like living here. It's just that Israel feels like our land. It's where we belong.

DEBORAH N

I love Hebrew. I think the Hebrew language is beautiful in itself, that's old Hebrew particularly. One phrase comes to mind from the daily prayer – sadly, people reading this will miss the lovely Hebrew words. It's 'You open your hand and satisfy the desire of every living thing', from one of David's Psalms.

Another of his Psalms which I like is 'The Lord is my shepherd'. In its Hebrew version, there's a beautiful tune which goes with it. Songs are sung at the different meals of Shabbat. 'The Lord is my shepherd' is sung typically at the last meal. It's melancholy. Very, very haunting and uplifting. The end of the Sabbath is approaching and we're sad because it's ending.

Actually, because Deborah likes it so much, we sing it on Friday night, when other people tend to sing something a bit more riotous!

JEREMY N

FACT-FINDER

David's Psalms
About half the Psalms (sacred songs) in the Book of Psalms in the Bible are said to have been written by King David. The two Jeremy mentions are numbers 145 and 23.

Shabbat
The Jewish Sabbath, lasting from sunset on Friday until sunset on Saturday.

The blessing 'Blessed art thou, O Lord our God, who has kept us alive, and maintained us, and made us reach this time' is said at the start of each festival in the Jewish year.

I find it particularly poignant. It focuses the mind on the passage of time, on similar festivals in the past, on family and friends absent for various reasons, on present joys, on recent difficulties, and on the fact that God *made* us reach that point in time.

Without God's help, the continuity that this represents would not exist. I'm mindful that it's not always certain I could do it by my own efforts.

SANDY L

There's one phrase which I say every day, several times a day. It's the Shema, the most important phrase in the Jewish religion: 'Hear, O Israel, the Lord our God, the Lord is One.'

It's important because it emphasizes monotheism, and belief in one God means unity. You could ask, 'Why all the fuss about the Israelites coming out of Egypt and building a golden calf?' Well, what they were doing was making a division, creating more than one God. If you have more than one God, you have more than one people. They'll always be opposed to each other.

So the Shema contains the few words that are in fact the most meaningful.

LOUIS M

FACT-FINDER

Israelites ... golden calf
The story of the making of the golden calf is told in Exodus 32 in the Bible.

I think the prayer which matters to me most is the one we say every day at the end of every service, Alenu.

I actually think that, as Jews, we say too many prayers. Praying is too automated. For example, the daily morning service takes thirty-five minutes. During it, I wonder how many people actually take in what they're saying, even if they speak Hebrew.

I don't like praying in the week with a minyan because it's too much of a circus. I like to pray in the privacy of my own home. At the end I say a prayer in English for my family. I prefer to say something which I understand and believe, rather than masses of Hebrew prayers I don't because I don't speak the language well enough.

But Alenu is understandable. I think it's an important prayer. To me, if Alenu were said on its own, perhaps with the Shema, it would be more meaningful than lots of prayers being said in the hubbub and commotion of a synagogue full of people rushing to get to work.

To me, it's better to say less and say it slowly.

EDDIE

I think, in a lot of situations that happen in life, I get the greatest comfort and find the most meaning and interest in the Psalms. There are Psalms appropriate to almost every situation.

EDNA M

FACT-FINDER

Alenu
Closing declaration of daily prayers that God is King over Israel and Lord of the universe.

Minyan
Literally 'count' (as in 'head count') or member. Certain public prayers, such as the Kaddish (see page 39), and public reading from a Torah scroll cannot take place without a minyan. In an Orthodox synagogue, this means having at least ten adult male Jews (i.e. aged thirteen or over) present.

Shema
'Hear, O Israel, the Lord our God, the Lord is One', the first sentence of the Shema, is the fundamental statement of Jews' belief in one God. The first paragraph goes on to state the central importance of Torah (Jewish Law). Orthodox Jews recite the Shema three or four times a day.

Psalms
A psalm is a sacred song or hymn. Edna means the psalms in the Book of Psalms in the Bible.

THINGS I FIND CHALLENGING

ne of the biggest challenges I face is that I'm a doctor and I have to work on the Sabbath.

Doctors have permission from the Chief Rabbi to work on the Sabbath. Not only are Jews allowed to break the Sabbath to save life, we *must* break the Sabbath to save a life. The difficulty, though, comes in the grey areas, where life isn't necessarily at risk.

I don't come from a background where I've always kept the Sabbath. That's something I came to slowly myself during my late teens. But now it's a way of life and breaking it's very, very difficult for me.

One way I overcome this is by changing ever so slightly what I normally do during the week. It's one of the things the rabbis suggest. For example, on the Sabbath I'll hold my pen with an extra finger. I'll wear my good clothes, because I don't normally wear my good clothes to work. This is called using a shenui. It's basically differentiating the Sabbath from the rest of the week, respecting it by behaving differently. I just do what I feel I can to respect the day.

At the moment I'm a hospital doctor. I want eventually to work in a GP practice, where I hope I'll be able not to have to work on the Sabbath.

JEREMY N

FACT-FINDER

Chief Rabbi
The Chief Rabbi (of Great Britain and the Commonwealth) is a learned man who has authority over a wide section of the Jewish community in Britain in matters of Jewish law.

I suppose not being able to do anything on the Sabbath means we miss lots of good programmes on television and lots of other things, too. But that's not really challenging. I'm used to it so it isn't really hard.

AMANDA L

When you're eight and you go to shul, you don't always understand what people are saying. So it's sometimes a bit hard to want to go.

LEONIE L

FACT-FINDER

Shul
Pronounced *shool*, this is the Yiddish word (see page 7) for 'synagogue'.

What I personally find the biggest challenge of my religious life is organizing things so that I can always get home on a Friday afternoon in time for the Sabbath.

Sabbath starts shortly before the sun sets, and this varies according to the time of the year and the country you're in. In Israel, it's always around six o'clock. Here it can start as early as half past three.

So I always have to make sure I leave enough time to get home, have a wash, get changed into nice clothes.

JEFFREY L

Being Jewish is a challenge, but you don't choose it. It's an accident of birth, if you like. I do feel a very heavy responsibility towards the heritage of being Jewish. I think I've felt that since I was quite a small child.

When the War broke out, I was nine. I was evacuated. I hadn't seen the countryside before because I was a town child. I hadn't been separated from my parents. I'd only come across Jewish people or non-Jews who were neighbours and friends.

When we were evacuated, it was a very different world. I first encountered anti-Semitism then, and it left a very big impression. In the village where we went, we were welcomed. We were given bags of sweets and things to make us feel at home. Then we were allotted to our billets. It was quite obvious the people we met knew we were Jewish and they really didn't expect us to be ordinary people. They really thought we were going to have horns. This was terrifying to me. I couldn't understand it.

FACT-FINDER

The War • Evacuated
During the Second World War, many town children in Britain were sent to live with country families to escape the German bombing raids.

Anti-Semitism
Anti-Jewish feelings and behaviour.

I think one of the very hardest things about being Jewish is being made to feel different wherever you are. Yes, I suppose we are different. But in so many ways we're not. We're people, like everyone else.

It isn't a difficulty now. I accept it. Nevertheless, there's a level at which I'm still sensitive. For instance, if I read or hear of a crime committed somewhere and a Jewish name is involved, that hits me. It seems so much worse, somehow. Strange, isn't it? I suppose in some way I'm sharing the responsibility.

EDNA M

T here are people we know who have Jewish ancestors and who are Jewish themselves but who haven't placed importance on having Jewish descendants. Jeffrey's family and mine are both very large ones. It's actually very sad to look around at our extended families and see who of our children's generation has any sort of a Jewish life.

Jeffrey's grandfather assumed that the next generations would learn the traditions and values of Judaism as he did. He assumed there would be a background of home and community and school all one and the same in their outlook and philosophy and objectives. It would happen as naturally as we breathe the air. It does still happen in certain communities which are able, rightly or wrongly, to shut out the outside world. I think the difficulty or the challenge is for us to balance the Jewish world with other influences in our lives. To get the balance right for our children and for ourselves.

SANDY L

I t's a great challenge to get through to people and give comfort to people when they are in trouble. Many people look to the rabbi for comfort.
Take today as an example.

A neighbour's son-in-law has died. He was thirty-six. Our neighbour's daughter asks would I please take the funeral because her rabbi is on holiday.
Of course I would.

My wife and I went this afternoon to a circumcision. It's a happy occasion. Not so happy for the baby, who's crying a little bit, but within twelve hours the operation is all forgotten. A child has been brought into the Covenant of Abraham. Before the circumcision he was born a Jew, yet he wasn't a complete Jew because he hadn't entered the Covenant. So there's a celebration. People come to the home of the baby for the ceremony. They drink a cup of tea or coffee or maybe a little whisky or wine, have a piece of cake. In very Orthodox homes it is customary to sit down to a meal.

But the grandmother of the baby has mixed emotions. Her father's just had a stroke. She has called me outside. She has tears in her eyes because of her father. So I have to find a way to comfort her, by balancing the anxiety over her father's illness against the joy of a new grandson.

From there, we went to visit another grandmother. We thought she'd be very happy because she'd just had a granddaughter. She's full of tears because she's had cross words with the daughter-in-law so she cannot visit the baby – a family complication which requires gentle counselling.

I also have to bring peace between a father and son who are at logger-heads. Because of their differences, the marriage of the parents is under great strain. I have to talk to the mother, the father and the son – separately and together.

These are the challenges. The rabbi has become not just the public figure who speaks in the synagogue but a social worker and counsellor much of the time. His role has changed as the generations have changed.

SIDNEY

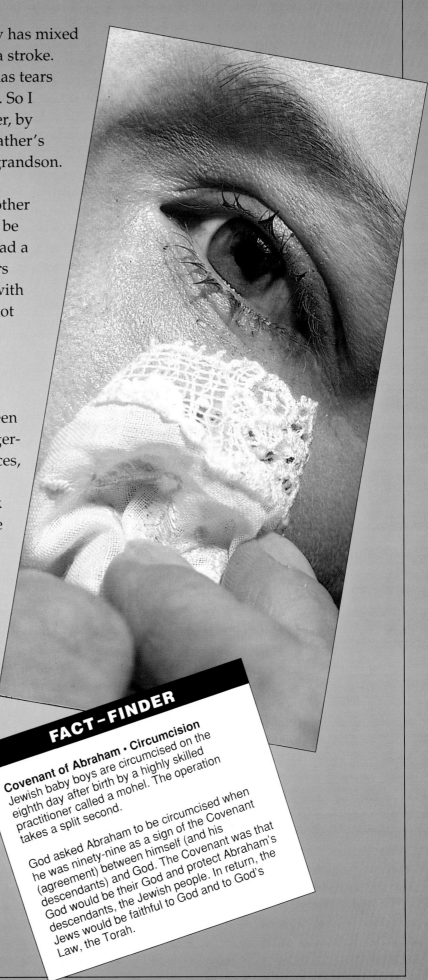

FACT-FINDER

Covenant of Abraham • Circumcision

Jewish baby boys are circumcised on the eighth day after birth by a highly skilled practitioner called a mohel. The operation takes a split second.

God asked Abraham to be circumcised when he was ninety-nine as a sign of the Covenant (agreement) between himself (and his descendants) and God. The Covenant was that God would be their God and protect Abraham's descendants, the Jewish people. In return, the Jews would be faithful to God and to God's Law, the Torah.

47

INDEX

Page numbers in **bold** type show where words or phrases are explained in FACT-FINDERS